I Dream in White Horses

Poems and Paintings

Giles Watson

© 2022 Giles Watson. All rights reserved.
ISBN 978-1-6781-9728-5

Ridgeway Awake

I need not sleep - to dream of them -
Those Ways that etch - in white -
Their trails between the Sky - and Earth -
The Ancients made - and walked -

I only need half-close one eye
To see the broomrape spike
Rise above the grassy verge -
And I can find - awake -

The Sign that points - toward the Hill -
And to the Stones - away -
Beside the Path that ever wends
Toward - eternal - Day -

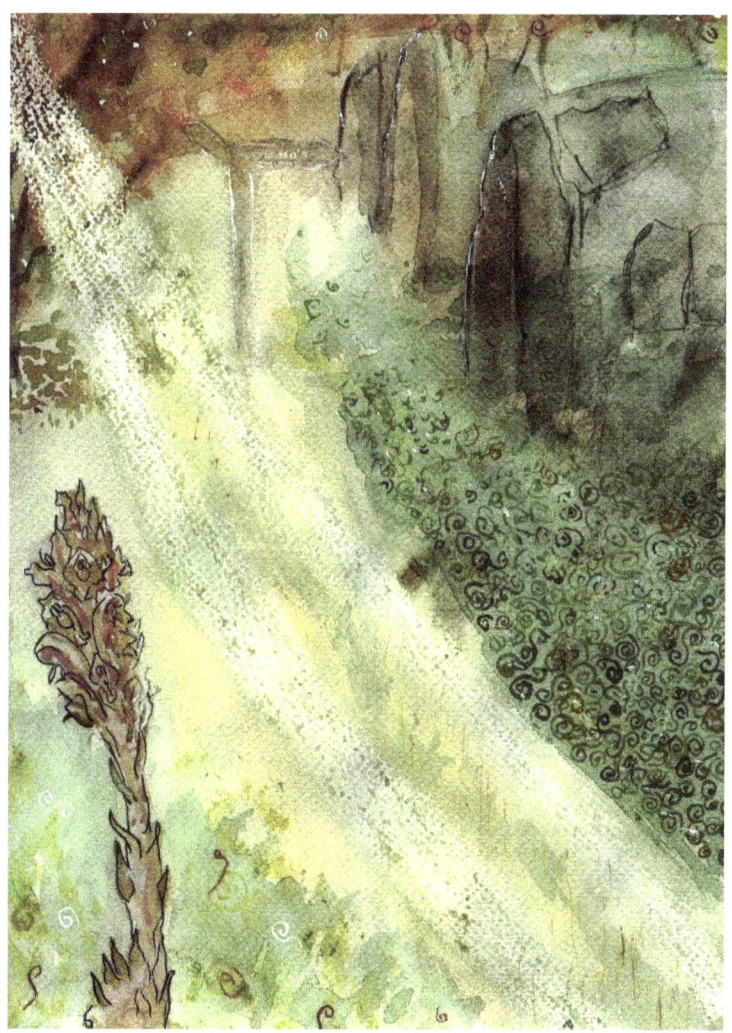

I Might Lose Myself

I might lose myself - in grass
Today among the Beeches -
Hide my self in quaking stems
Beneath the summer branches -

I hope to hear the Cuckoo - so
I may return - next year -
Whether she's above my head
Or echoing - afar -

I hope to hear the Cuckoo - for
There's gravity - in Stones
That draws me as a moth - to Light
And kindles - my young bones -

Something that's renewed - each year
With the Solstice Sun -
That keeps my spirits - frolicking
When Winters are - so wan -

I might be a splash - of tint -
Demarcating - sky -
But Stones are older far - than paint
And solider - than I -

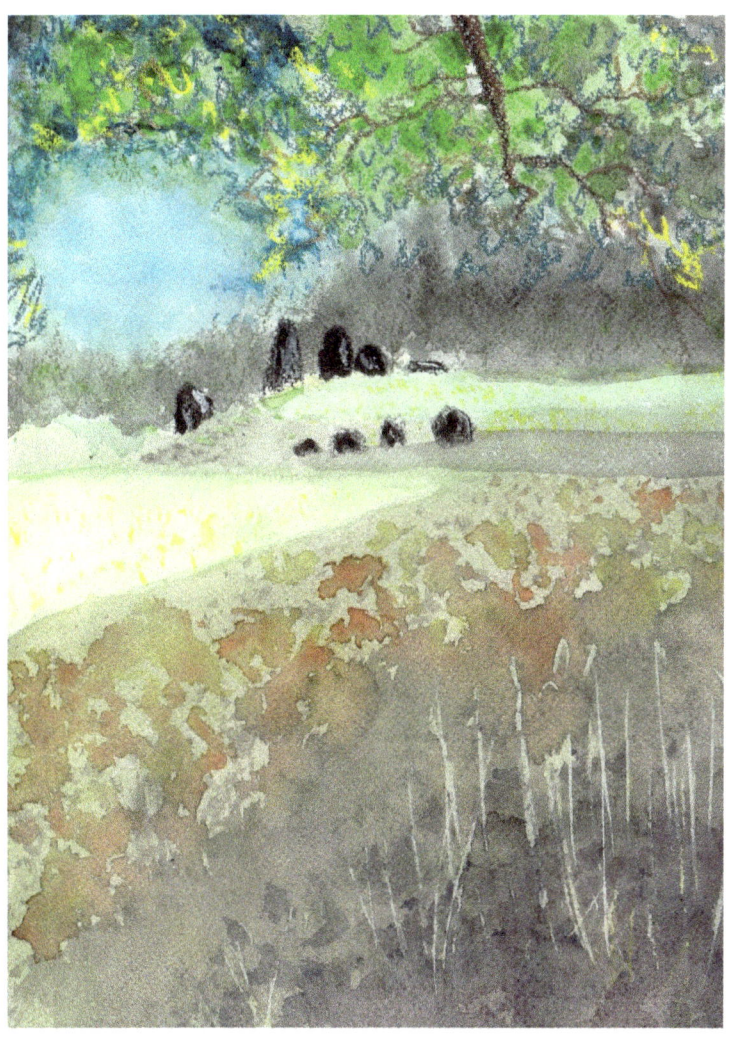

Sketching Wayland's Smithy

In shadows cast by beeches
I smudge my coloured chalk
To draw the depth - of shadows -
Leave white - the solid rock -

For shadow here - has substance
Tangible - as stone -
My hands all bruised - with shadow
By the time - I'm done -

My legs grown numb with kneeling
Amid the fallen mast -
An aching - in my fingers -
Foretells - a coming mist -

But this bare patch - of paper
Remembers - my delight
When sunlight filtered sideways
And seared the Sarsens - white -

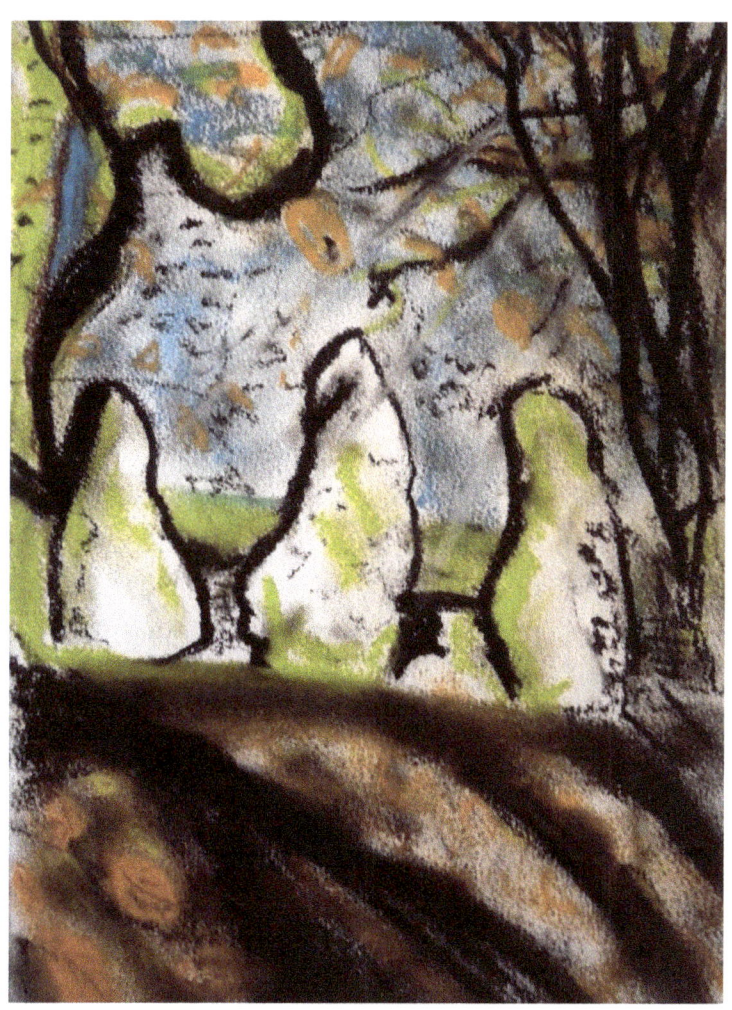

The Meadow-Drain

Where the footpath meets the road
There is another Way -
It flows beside - and underground -
Always wending - by -

Ignored except when Celandines
Are trumped - by Daffodils -
Out-yellowed by Marsh Marigolds
With roots that seek - the rills -

I've walked along the Meadow-Drain
Through quag and barbed-wire fence
In quest to know - where water goes -
I met a grass-snake - once -

And she was hunting - after frogs -
The Meadow-Drain - her World -
Lithe among the Celandines -
Electric - to behold -

She lives where yellow lights the eye
And water is - a god -
I never tramp unheeding now
Where footpath meets - the road -

II

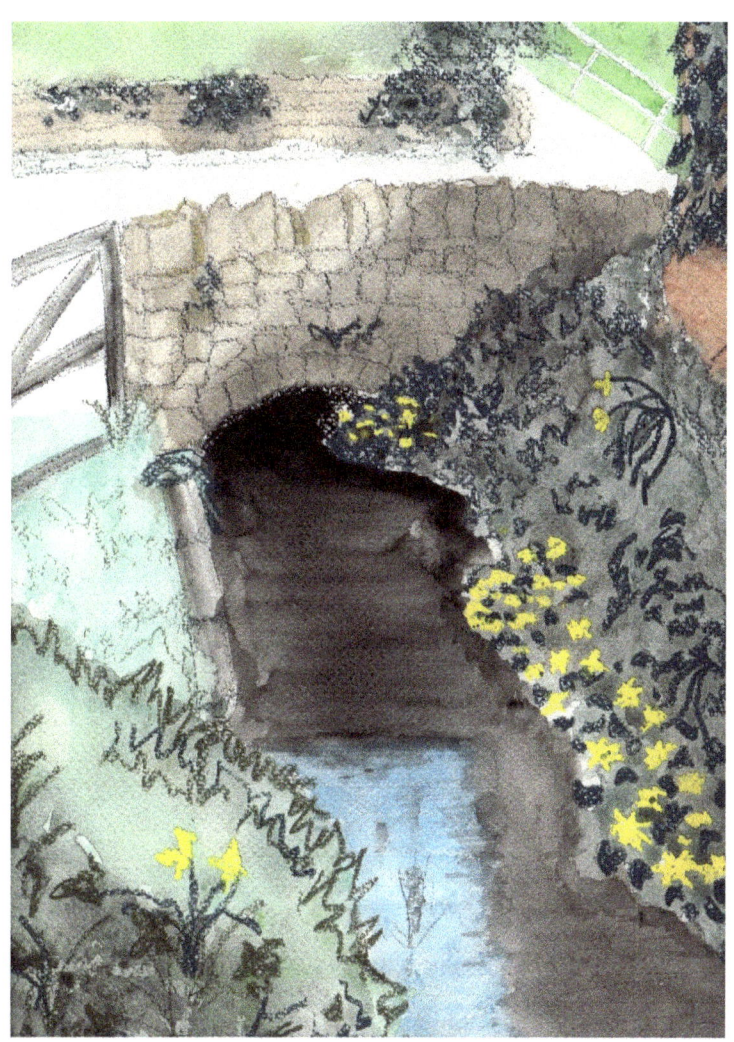

A Trick of Light

I seek the shaft of winter light
That keeps the Year - awake -
Not one leaf - upon a Beech -
The barbed-wire fence hangs - slack -

And I imagine Campions -
A trick of Light - or Time -
They flare - a moment - in the shade
To keep the Margins - warm -

The stones and trees are algal green
Though sap is hiding - deep -
The Earth - herself - a sepulchre
Whose spectral Flowers - sleep -

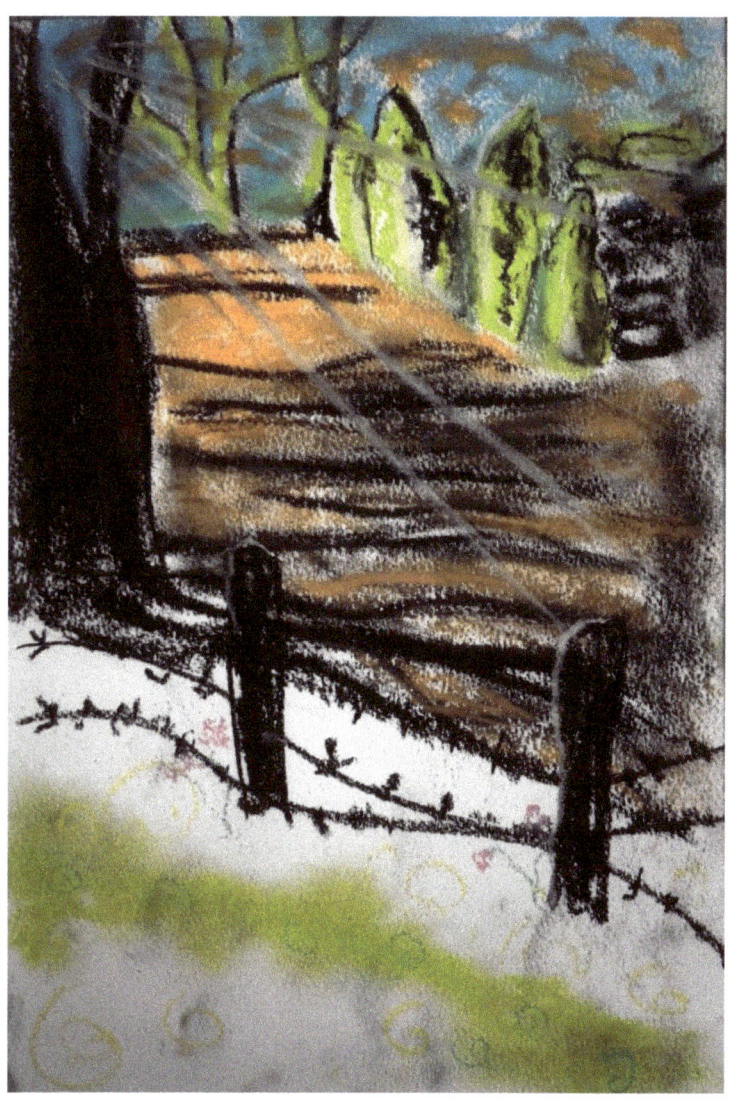

Winter Light

When sunlight floods the Smithy
I look to where the mound
Tapers - to the beeches -
And dispossess - my mind -

These elongated shadows
Cast by winter sun
Turn trees - to constellations
Make alidades - of stone -

I read the declination
Of descending light -
I sharpen - all my senses -
Yet set myself - at nought -

For I am - only feeling
And present - as a ghost
Is present - in a yearning
When everything - is lost -

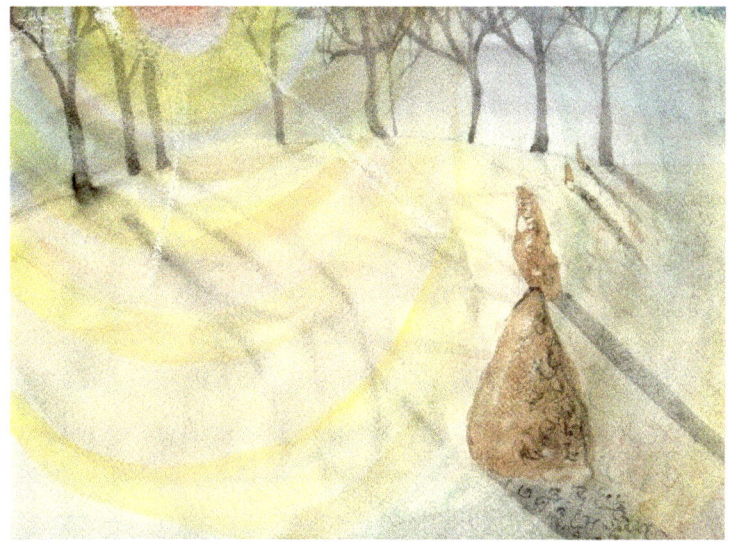

Signpost in the Winter Light

Signpost in the winter light
When everything's - afire -
And the chalk is hard with ice -
You fork and point - afar -

One Way goes to White Horse Hill -
One to Wayland's Smithy -
One leads between a farm and woods
Where scents are dark and earthy -

And I have taken all of these
A thousand times - and more -
When the glow-worms lit the way
Colder far - than fire -

And when the stubble wears to dust
Or torrents melt - the Clod -
I shall walk - though quite alone -
A path that is - well trod -

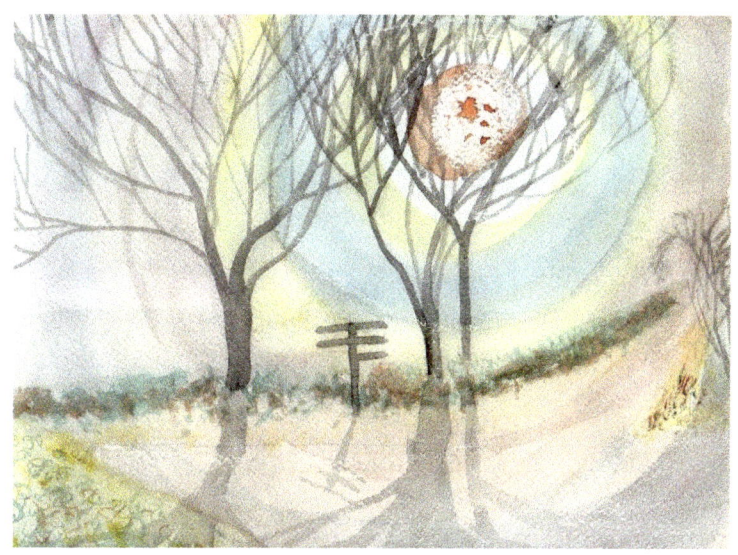

Beyond the Canola Field

The Ridgeway is a corridor
Where the wild things thrive
Through the fields where oil-seed rape's
The only thing alive

But I can wander sideways
By hedge or woodland ride
To find the Thrush's anvil
Or setts where Badgers hide

And turn with spirits joyful
Up the way of trampled chalk
Where Campions are blushing
And tremble on their stalks

With Yellowhammers glinting
Through Hawthorns and through Sloes
Which lean above the pathway
Where a gale in winter blows

And watch the Skylark spiring
A mile away from harm
To forget - amid the ramparts -
The barren factory-farm -

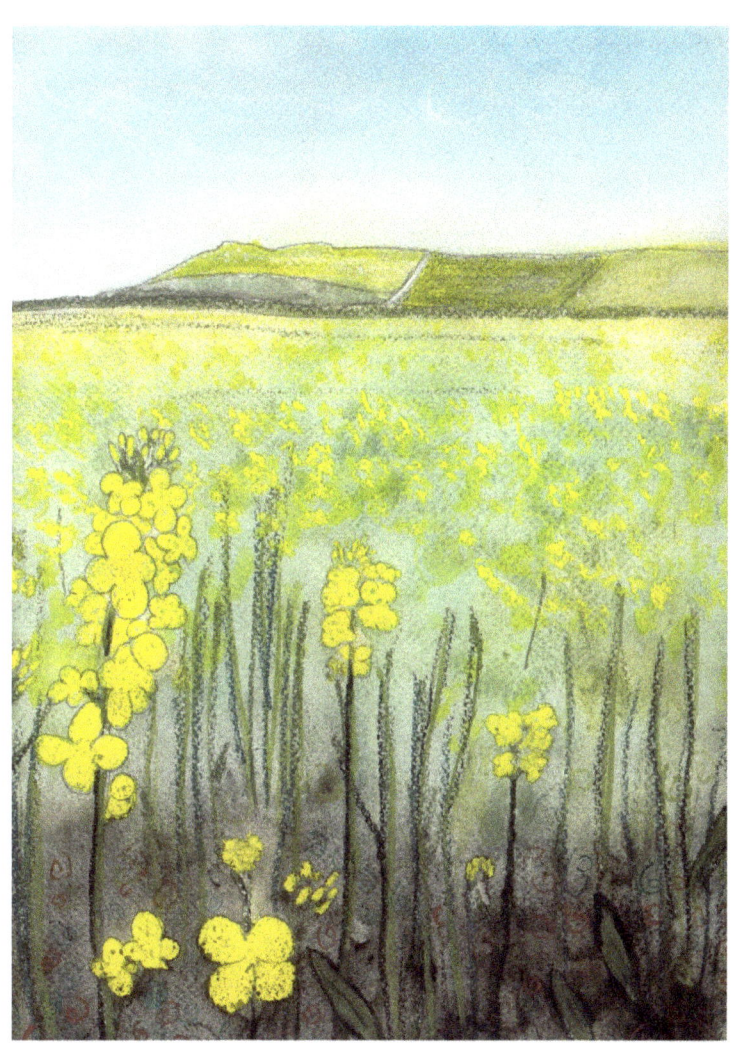

Falling Beech Tree

I trespassed - in a Hanger
After a great Storm
Loam - was heaved asunder
Lumps of Flint - were strewn -

Ivy clung to Branches
Roots impaled the Mist -
The way was blocked by Saplings -
Strewn with fallen Mast -

Soil - yawned before me -
A Gust - tore out my Breath -
I froze before the gaping
Interior - of Earth -

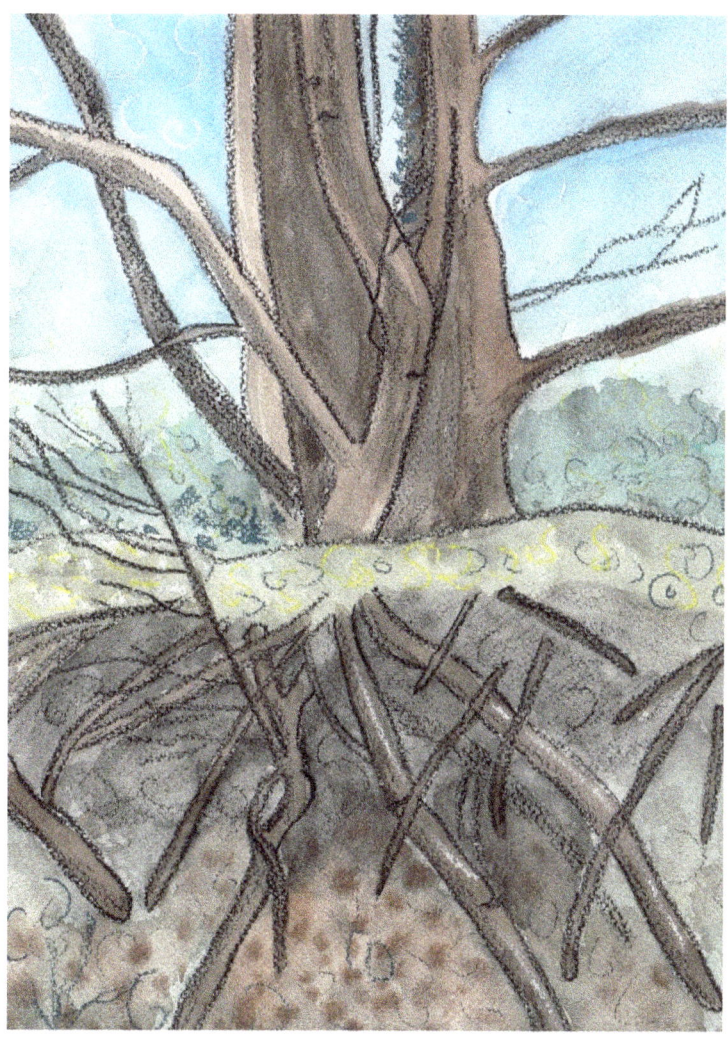

Beech Trees in Autumn

Beech trees wear an algal bloom
To smooth their arching limbs
Crowns against slow-shifting clouds
Roots - in ancient loams -

They let their twigs form traceries
That cross - and quest - and sweep -
Or cast their shadows - spindle-thin
Upon the Barrow-slope -

With leaves that dwindle every day
Taken by a Breeze
To cloak the ground with rustlings
And brush my heart - with Bronze -

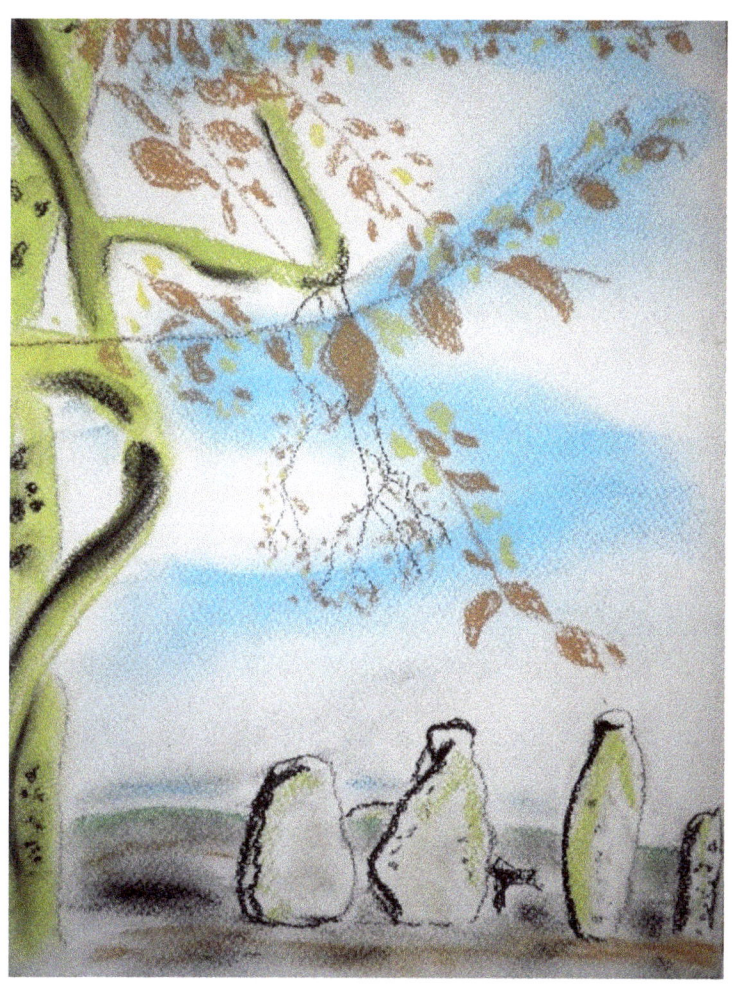

Roots of Avebury

Roots of beeches span the Earth
At Avebury - in leafy shade -
Encase the rampart - clutch and fuse
Solid - where the green boles stand -

As though they simmered - out of loam -
Solidified - and held
The Soil in a loving grip
Nurturing the Mould -

Folding - in their slow embrace
The antler pick and stone
Waiting for some heaving Birth -
Or for an Age - to turn -

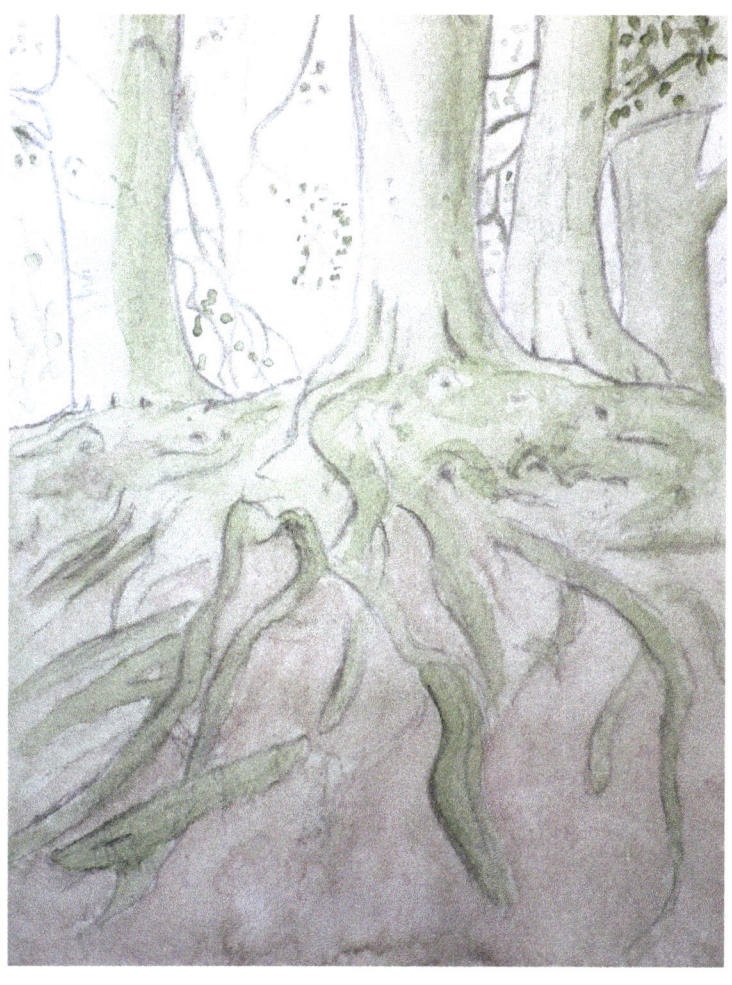

The Sentry-Tree

I stand before the Sentry-Tree
My senses on a tilt -
My heart - in time of leaflessness -
Waits for frost - to melt -

The Tree leans out as if to grip
The Sarsens in its clutch -
I sense that I am growing roots
To ground me - in my watch -

And algae stain the sigilled trunk
Sap green - where the Sun
Stirs the soul of chlorophyll -
Emergence is - begun -

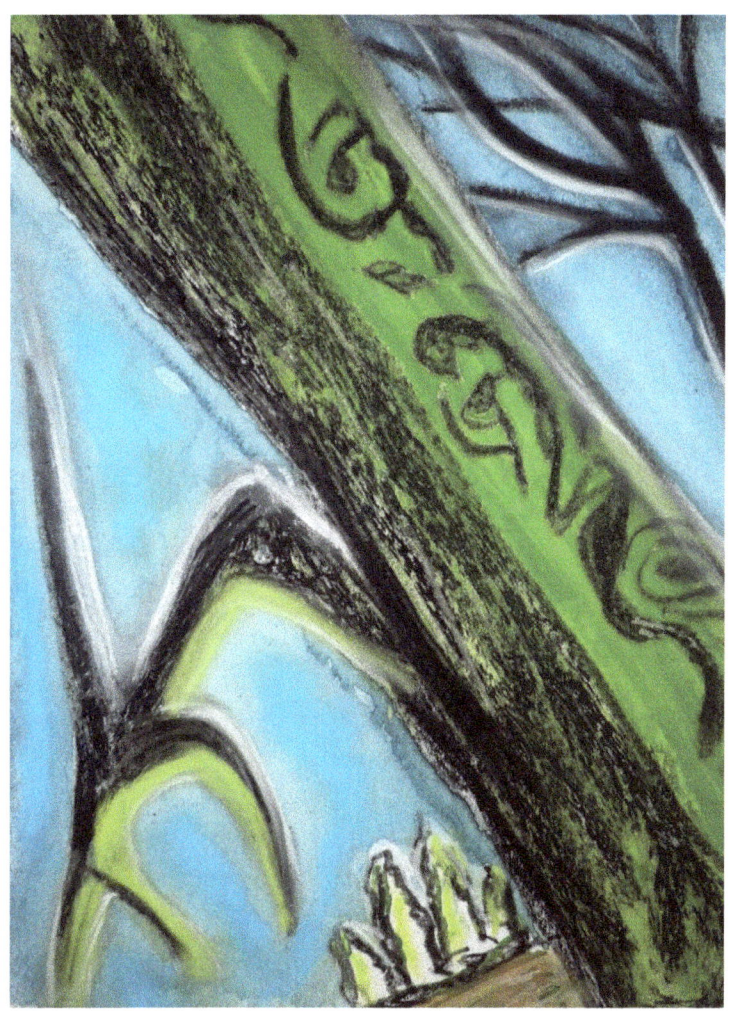

Hollow Ash

When this was a sapling
A squirrel gnawed - the stem
Or perhaps a bough - came down
And snapped it - in a storm -

Accidental coppice -
Sculpted by - a Wind -
Seeking yet - the sunlight
Sprouting - from the wound -

And opening - a yawning -
A gape - where snails hide -
Where autumn leaves are rotting -
They blew here - down the ride -

I stare into the fissure -
The darkness - damp and good -
Beckons me - forever
Within this Heart - of wood -

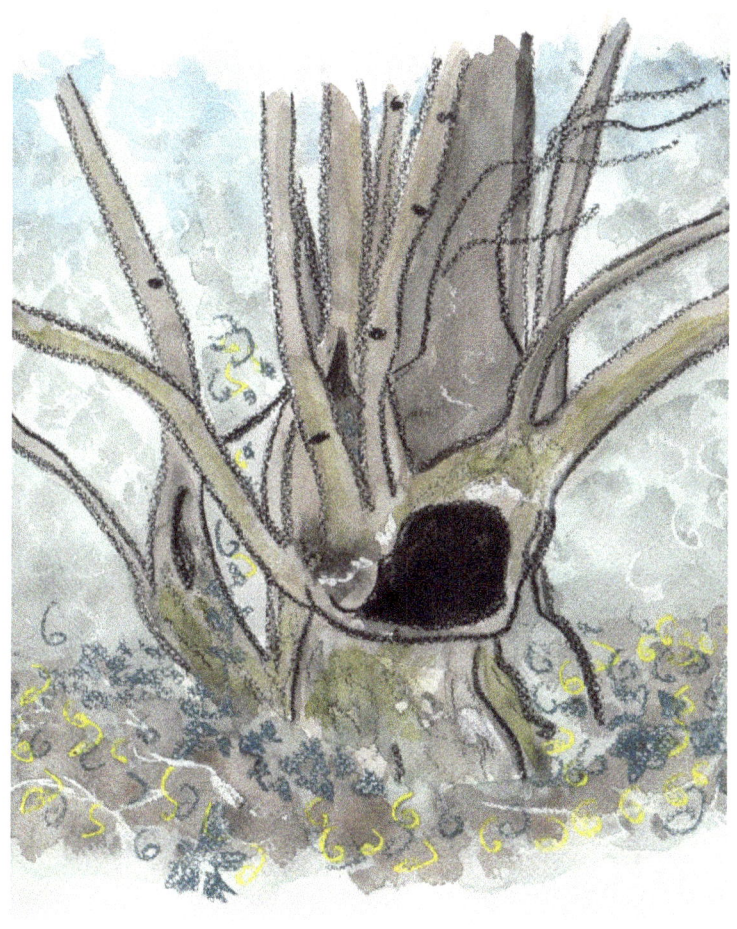

Hangman's Stone

I heard the Curlew by Crog Hill -
The orchids going over -
Uncanny voice of Wilderness
Lamenting from - Forever -

The Curlew called and I walked - on
Through the tufted vetch -
I found a path - between the fields -
A Buzzard perched - to watch -

Hedges closed - both sides about -
Above my head - they hung -
The Curlew's voice began - to fade -
The chalky path - was long -

And when the path began to curve
And chaffinches to fly -
Wearing lichens green and grey
The Hangman's Stone - stood by -

I turned beside the Hangman's Stone
And looked back - down the Way -
The Curlew's throat was silent now -
The Buzzard - flown away -

Hangman's Stone - Hangman's Stone -
With brambles - overgrown -
Long you lean - until the Day
When Everything - has flown -

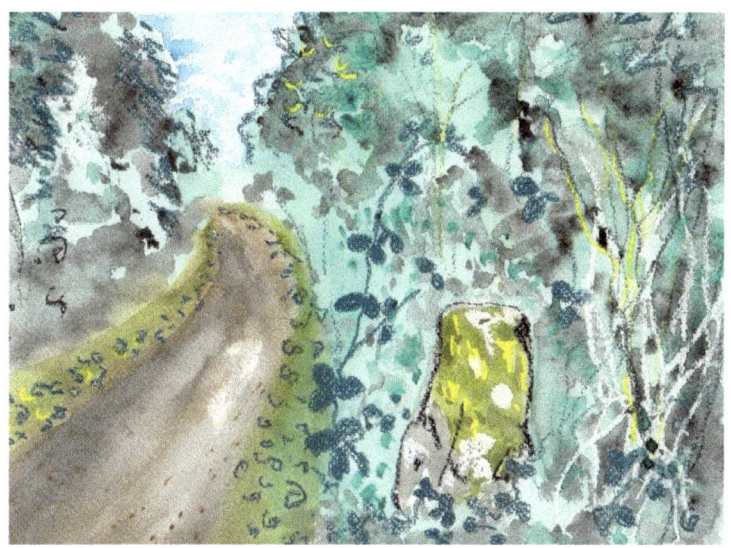

She Conceives a Landscape

She conceives - a Landscape
More water - than of soil
Seeking - after oceans
Beyond our human - scale

Pooling - after rainfall
Welling - underground
Emerging - into daylight
Knowing - where to wend

Curving - round the Sarsens
Silvered - by the Day
Merging - into Kennet
Seeking land - to splay

Seeping - into Meadows
Round the pregnant - Hill
She conceives - a Landscape
Water - makes it - swell -

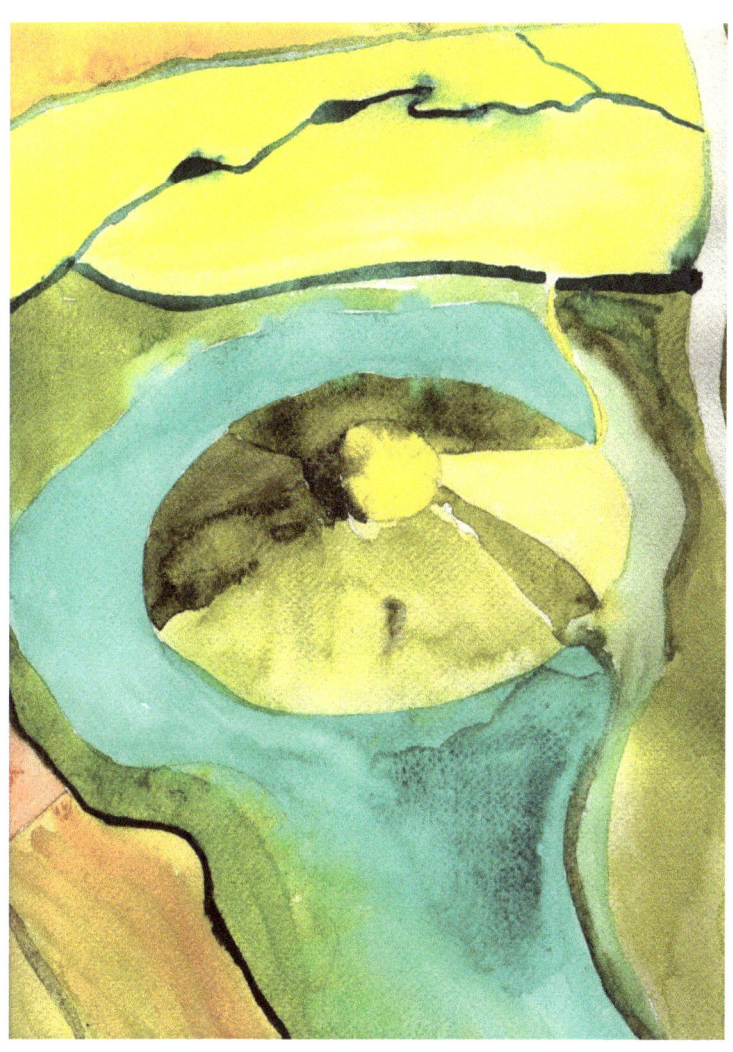

The Smithy in a Leaf

I see the Smithy in a Leaf
Its shadows cast - in veins -
It rides on eddies - to the soil -
Dries to bronze - as Autumn turns -

I see a leaf - I see a Flint
Chipped in facets - for a blade -
I see a line - of dappled Stones
Shadowing - the glade -

I see the Stones - I find the Leaf -
I hear the knapping of the Flint
Shadows - draw me to the cool -
Whispering - where Summer went -

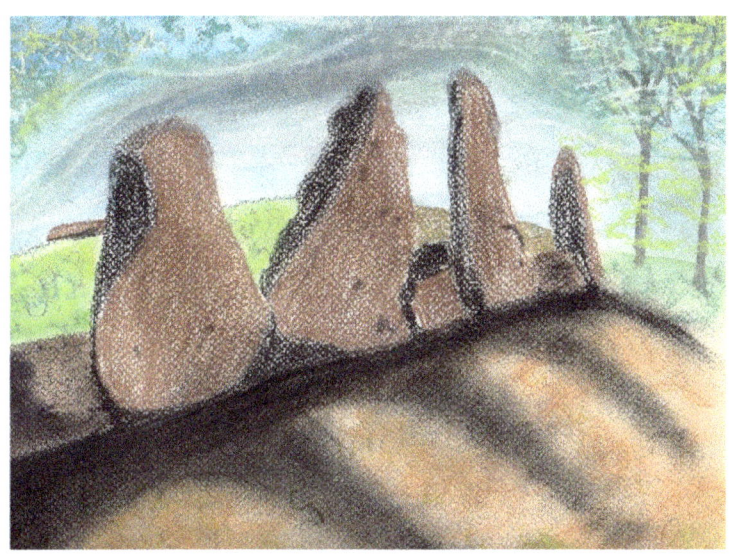

Ragged Robins

Where the ground grew quaggy
By a marge of Loosestrife
I found the Ragged Robins
In a cloud of teeming - Life -

Tiger Moths were flitting
And tandem-damselflies
A Hawker and a Darter
With gleaming Orbs - for eyes -

Upon a leaf - a Scorpion Fly
Curled its rose-thorn tail -
Butterworts and Lady's Smock
Edged out - to the Trail -

And high above them - tattered pink -
Nodding Robin's heads
To prove that Beauty's transient
And sometimes lives - in shreds -

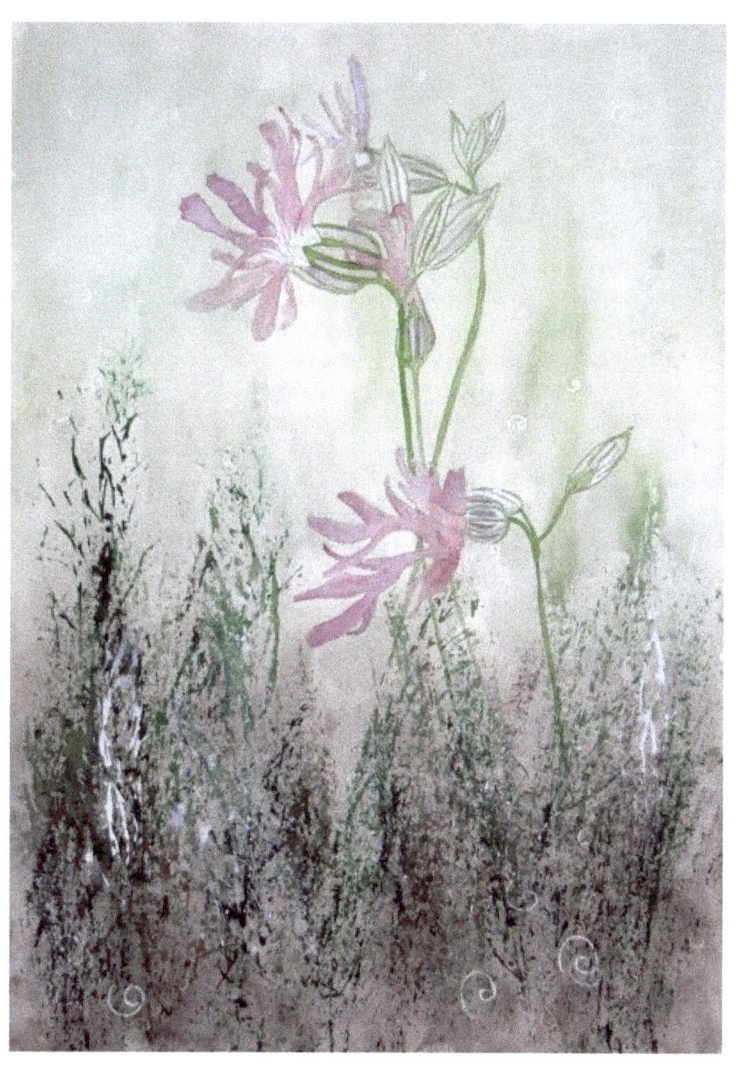

Lady's Smocks

Wide wet meadow
Making our beds
A hoverfly's landing
Bending our heads

Friends to the Adder
Pick and be bitten
Lie down amongst us
And be smitten

Pink as the dusk
Fading to mauve
Smocks of milkmaids
Blooming for love

Nodding in dewfall
Bent by a breeze
Come with the Cuckoo
Go when she flees

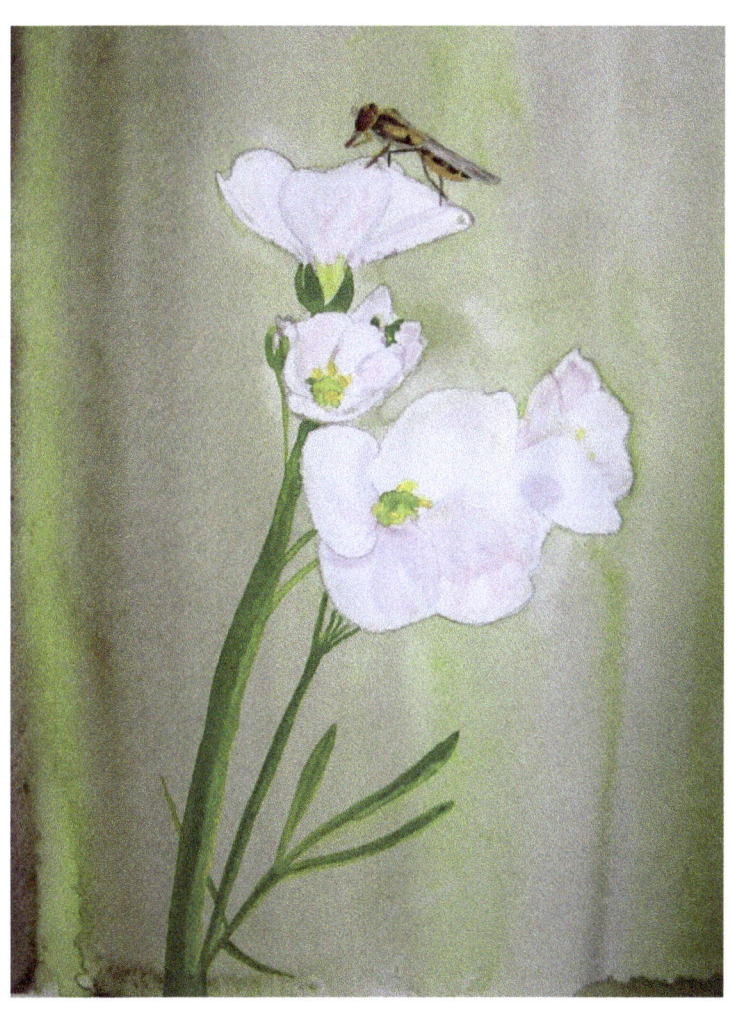

Herb-Robert

Robin redbreast lies a-bleeding -
Man - he killed him all for nought
While Herb-Robert was a-seeding -
Killed him - all for winter sport -

Robin redbreast - blood a-clotting
On the ground where Robert lies -
Robin redbreast - flesh a-rotting
Feeds the humus - feeds the flies -

Feeds the seed - Herb-Robert sleeping
Through the hour when Wrens are kings -
Robin's rosy blood is seeping
Up the shoots - when comes the spring -

Robert lies on ground a-bleeding -
Bloodstained petals - ruddy shoot -
Man - he dug him up a-weeding -
Exposed to air his withered root -

Man, he cannot bear the thought
Of any beast that chews the cud -
Such a curse has Robin wrought
All their milk has turned to blood -

Man no more shall Robin kill
His blood upon the ground - to sow -
No more wish Herb-Robert ill -
But grant he is a good-fellow -

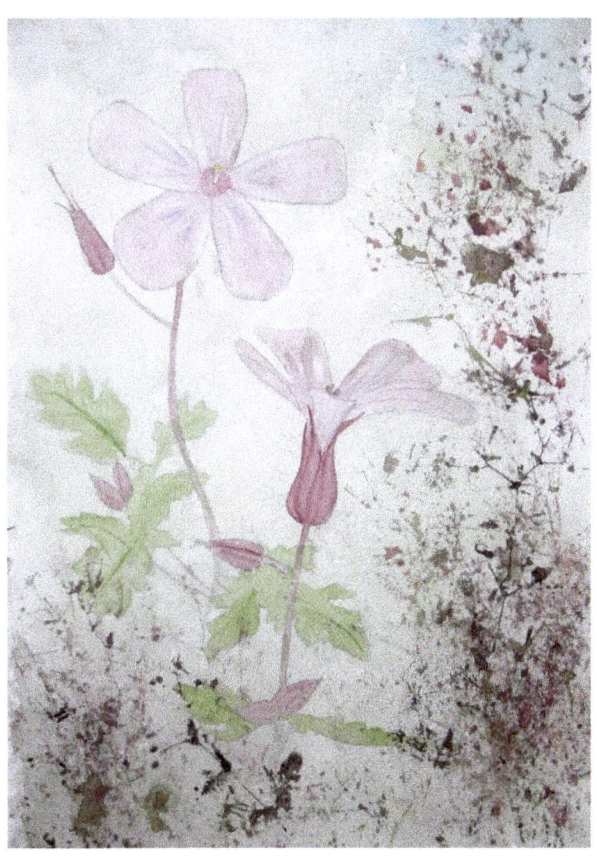

Campion Summer

That summer brought forth campions
Richer pink - in shade -
By paths upon the spines - of hills -
By tow-paths - woodland rides -

For oak grew catkins early -
Ash buds bursting - late -
A saturating springtide
Made summer more - complete -

Butterflies - flew vibrant -
The sky - took care - of them -
And concentrated colour
Quaked - on every stem -

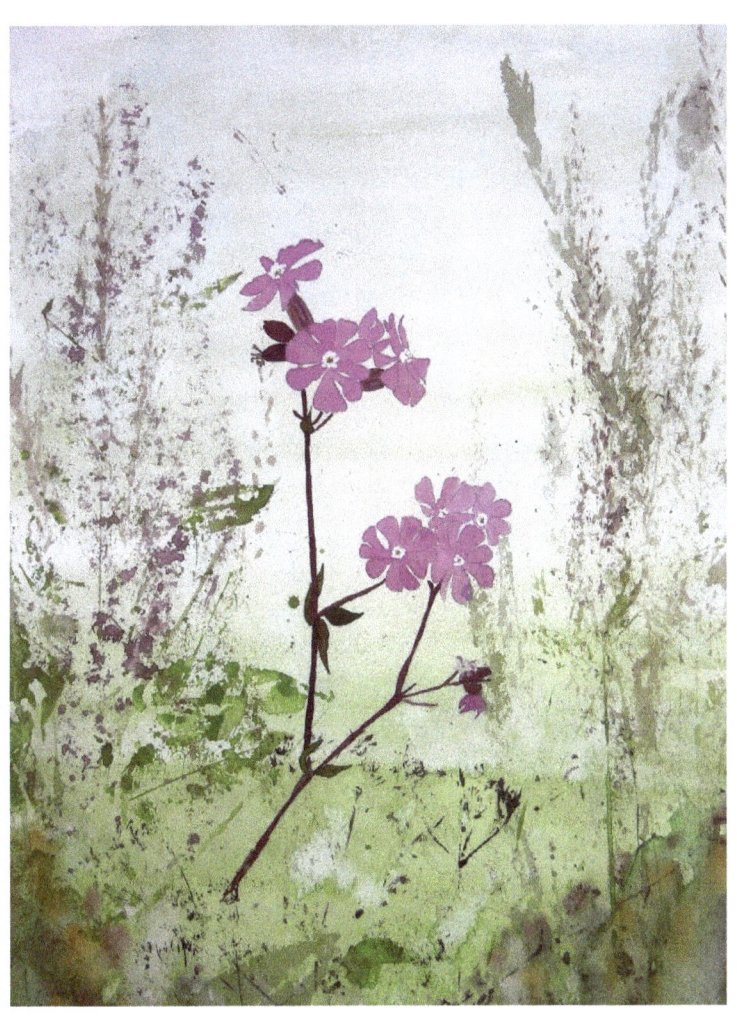

Hollyhocks in the Vale

They lift their heads as if to point
My way up - to the Downs -
These gladnesses - of Hollyhocks -
Freed - by meadow-drains -

Escaping gardens - cheese-wrapped seeds
Within the crops of birds -
Serried English prettiness
Breaking out - of bounds -

Of older ways - they seem to sing -
Not thrushes - but of Throstles -
On impulse - shake their petals loose
And dance - amid the thistles -

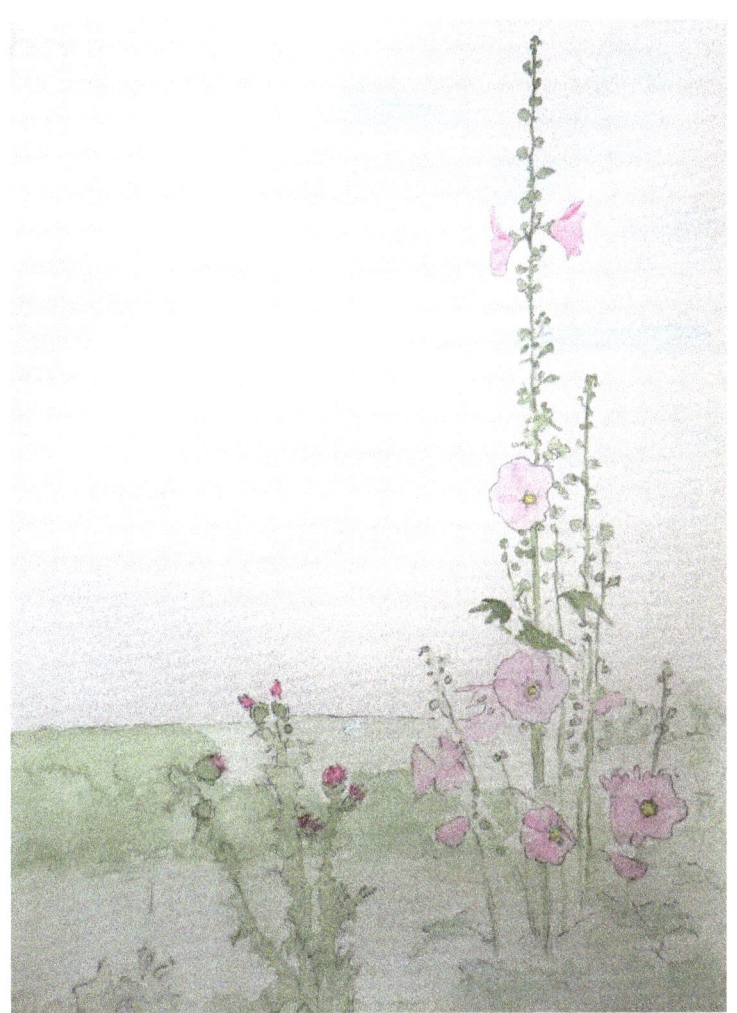

Fly Agaric

I know a wood of Birches
With boles blessed - by the Moon -
Whose trunks stand hollow - after Death -
With all their heartwood - gone -

Standing yet - but only bark -
Ice-caked in the cold -
But Autumn heaves the twigs and leaves -
A Sovereignty- of Mould -

When the bleach-white Volva splits
Vermilion thrusts - her head -
Dominion - parts the leaves of ferns -
The Queen - of all the Dead -

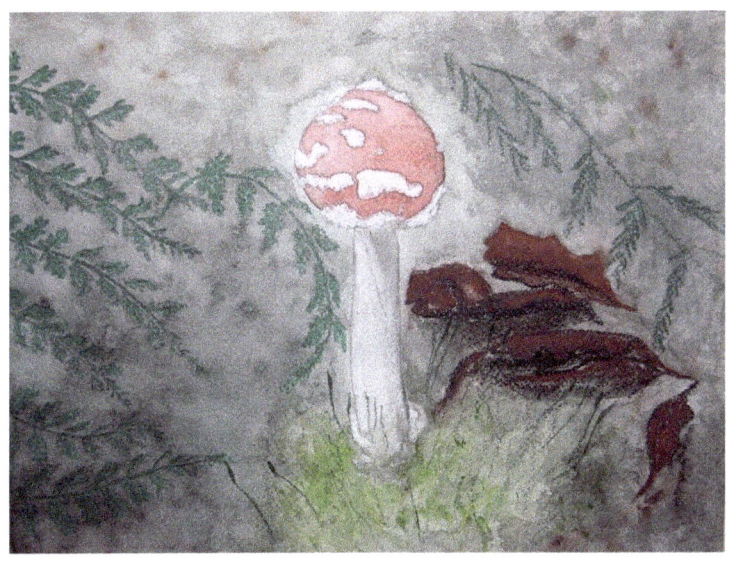

Roebuck

I must have been downwind of him -
He lingered - by the arch
Of beeches touching - at the twigs -
And stayed - awhile - in reach -

He curved his spine to gaze around
And watched - while all was Now -
Where arching shadows leaned across
The turnings - of the plough -

I might have touched his velvet flank
Or smelt his humid breath
Before he turned - as calm - as clouds -
And melted - into Earth -

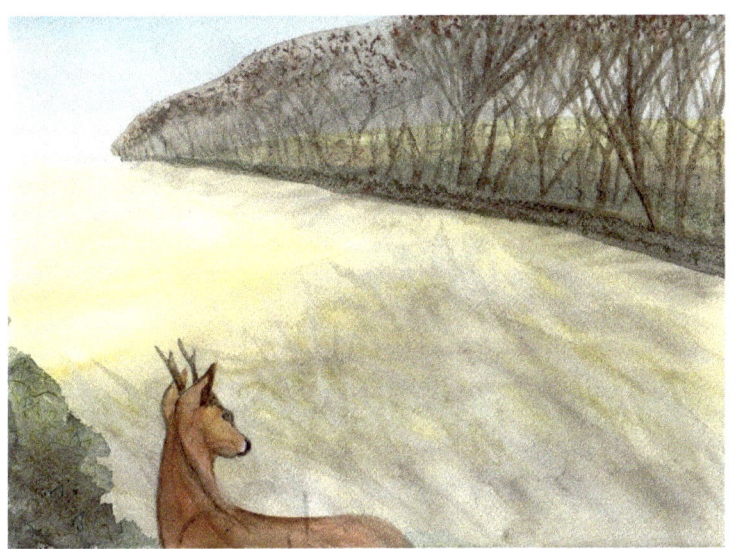

The Dog - the Roebuck - and the Lapwing

The murmur in my Lurcher's heart
Could be heard across the room -
I walked with him on Knighton Hill
When Heartsease was in bloom -

The Lapwing looped above the chalk
And whistled - where he went -
While I pleaded - to the earth -
And on my breath - a chant -

Heartsease - give my Lurcher health -
The Roebuck stopped and stared -
Unblinking in the open field -
Heeding - how we fared -

Heartsease - give my Lurcher health -
I gave the ground my tears -
My Lurcher pulled me - to the path -
And grinned - and leapt the years -

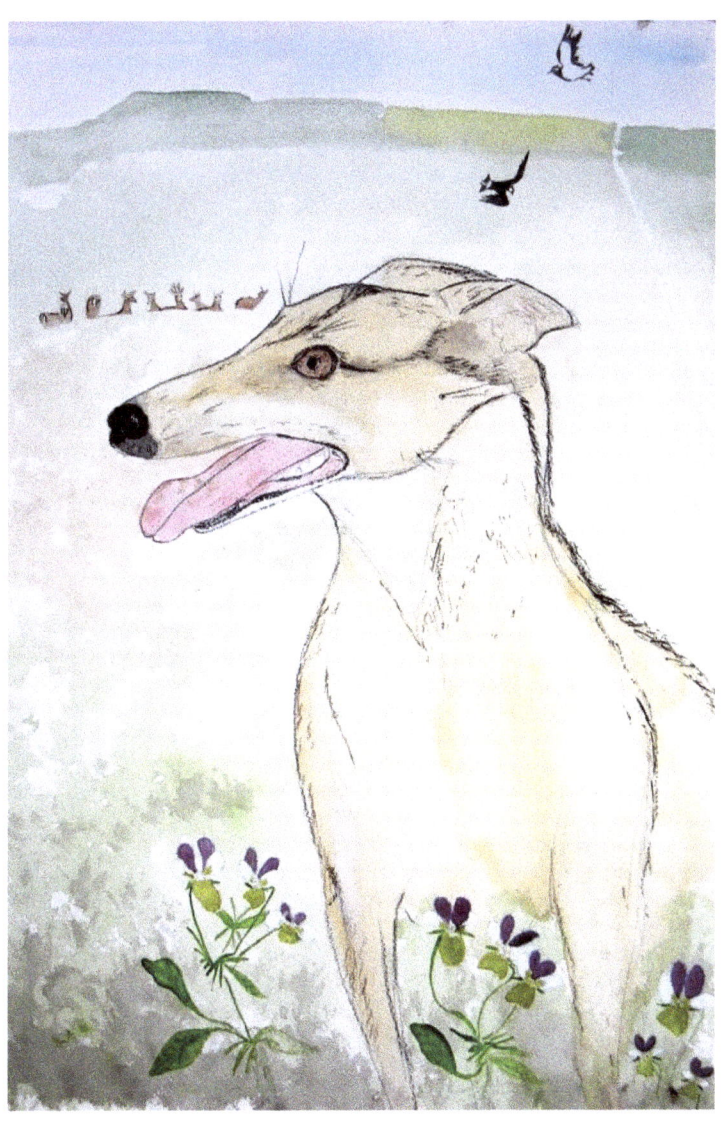

Downland Snails

By winter they've climbed the thistles and umbels -
sequestered themselves for sleep
in spirals - enwombed - where the wind trembles
a tangle of stems on the slope -

in shells they secreted from their own mantles -
calcium - gleaned from the chalk -
by summer - created - sheltered - by mottles -
tentative - tender - awake -

now they're all dormant - shrunk - into kernels
retracted - and numb to all else
but the long winter moment frozen in runnels -
deep within - barely - a pulse -

I might have retracted all that is tenderest -
hunkered it deep - into shell
to hold it protected - yet I am surest
to bear the brunt - when I am - still -

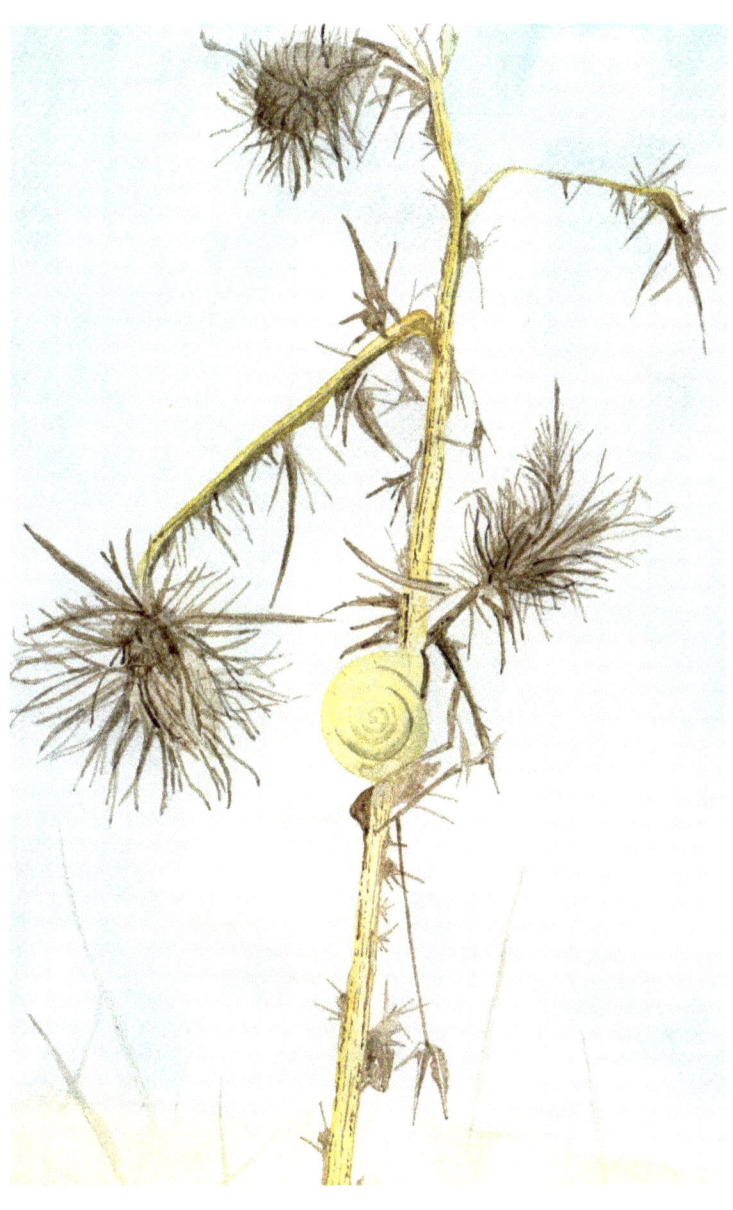

Comma

She lies awake - on leaf in curl
Her mottles - to the Sun
But a tiny - twitch of wing
Permits her - to be seen -

She bears her punctuation-mark
Upon her under-side -
It might be a mote - of dust -
A fleck - or curling seed -

I have learned by her advice
To hide my commas - well -
And imitate a withered leaf
In town eluding - all -

To flit out where the Way is white
A Period - too brief -
A little Breath - to quake my wing -
Or mark my Clause, of Life -

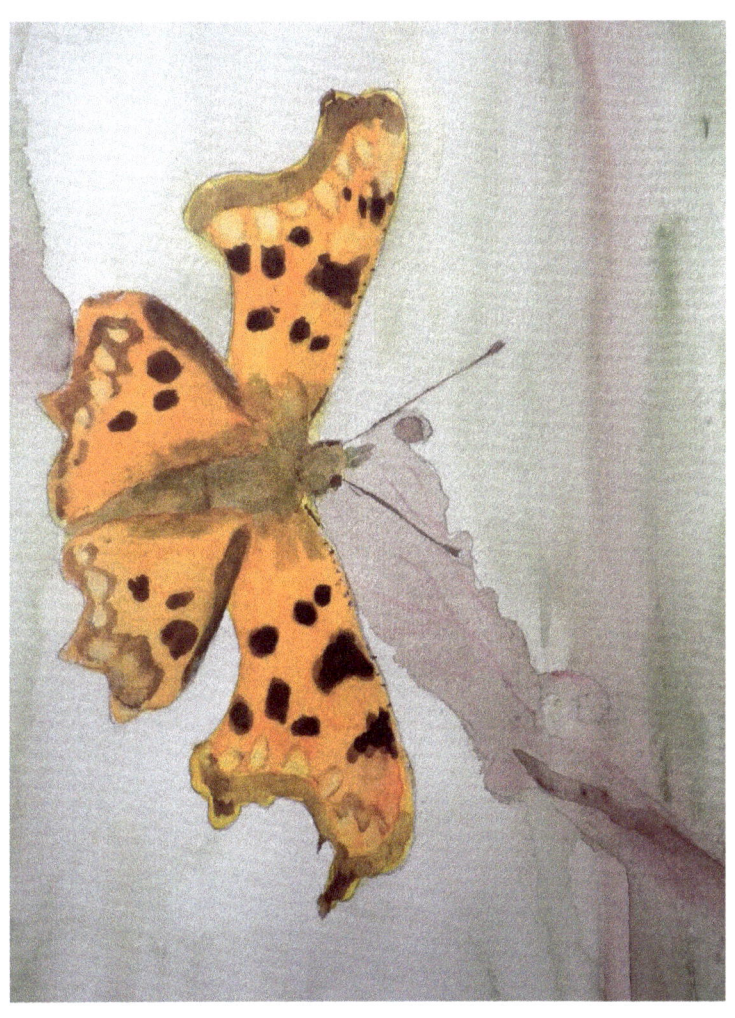

Scarlet Tiger

I caught a glimpse - of scarlet
By the path - above the moss
Where butterworts were flowering
And runnels formed - a maze -

I followed in his flitting
But somehow still - he flipped
As if he ceased - existing -
Or his Flash - was dreamt -

I crept amid the reedmace
And found him - on a leaf -
His wings a dart - and folded
To treasure - all his Life -

I hoped to catch - his crimson
But have no more - to tell -
I didn't dare disturb him -
Perhaps he sits there - still -

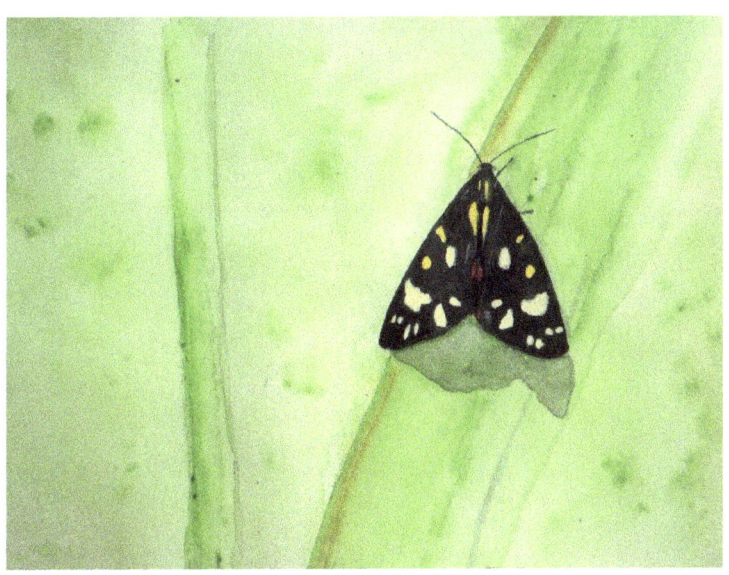

I Dream in White Horses

I dream in White Horses
Pacing out - over Heights
With Chalk for their bodies
And Fossils - for Hearts -

Flexing their Fetlocks -
Launching up - and away -
Pale living Etchings
On Landscapes - of Joy -

I dream in White Horses
Afar from the Town
Who leap - into Distance -
And never come - down -

The Lark calls me skyward
As clear as a Lake -
I dream in White Horses
And never - awake -

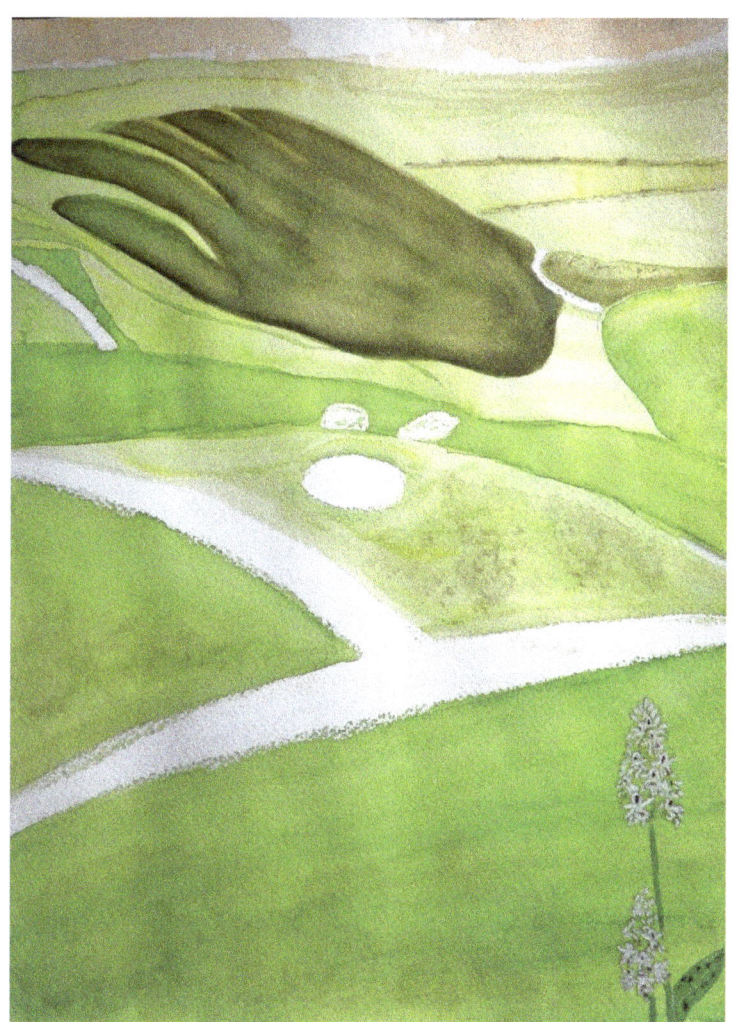

www.ingramcontent.com/pod-product-compliance
Lightning Source LLC
Chambersburg PA
CBHW040522220526
45473CB00013B/2951